ICED WATER

John Unrau

salmonpoetry

Published in 2000 by
Salmon Publishing Ltd,
Cliffs of Moher, Co. Clare, Ireland
http://www.salmonpoetry.com
email: info@salmonpoetry.com

Copyright © John Unrau 2000
The moral right of the author has been asserted.

A catalogue record for this book is available from the British Library.

The Arts Council
An Chomhairle Ealaíon Salmon Publishing gratefully acknowledges the financial assistance of The Arts Council/An Chomhairle Ealaíon.

Salmon Publishing also gratefully acknowledges the support of Atkinson College, York University, Toronto, in the publication of this book.

ISBN 1 903392 00 4 Paperback

All rights reserved. No part of this publication may be reproduced or transmitted in any form or by any means, electronic or mechanical, including photography, recording, or any information storage or retrieval system, without permission in writing from the publisher. The book is sold subject to the condition that it shall not, by way of trade or otherwise, be lent, resold or otherwise circulated without the publisher's prior consent in any form of binding or cover other than that in which it is published and without a similar condition, including this condition, being imposed on the subsequent purchaser.

Cover design by Brenda Dermody
Set by Siobhán Hutson
Printed by Techman Ireland Ltd., Dublin

Acknowledgements

Special thanks to Linda McNamara for constant encouragement, and much help in shaping these poems for publication.

Acknowledgements are due to the editors of the following, in which some of these poems first appeared:
Descant, the new renaissance, Queens Quarterly, Scrivener, Wascana Review, New Quarterly, Indigo, The Ruskin Newsletter, paper flowers for foil figures, Poetry Ireland Review, The Honest Ulsterman, and *The Salmon.*

Also to the editors of the annual anthologies of the League of Canadian Poets entitled *Garden Varieties, More Garden Varieties, Vintage 93, 94, 95, 97,* and the annual anthology of the Atkinson Poetry Circle entitled *A View on the Garden.*

Contents

Father	1
Walking Home To Mayfair, January 1928	3
Black Sunday, April 14th, 1935	5
Untitled	6
Winter Day Near Etzikom, Alberta	7
Brother Drychthelm of Melrose	8
Cindy with the News from Sky	10
Celebrated Visiting Poet	11
Field Mouse And Grey Owl	12
Old Maggie On The High Level Bridge	13
On Lake Agnes Trail	14
Drylands Storm	15
Evangelical Aunt	16
Suburban Grave	17
Hoeing The Old Woman's Garden	18
New-Age Muskie Considers A Change Of Lifestyle	19
St. Hugh, Bishop of Lincoln	21
Dirty Old Man, Edmonton Schoolyard	23
To Wordsworth, From Ontario	24
Bereavement	27
Sanctuary	29
Counterparts	30
Angina Poem	32
The Eternal Feminine In Art	34
Mosquitoes: Etzikom, Alberta, 1918	36
Whitemud Devotions	37

On The Old CPR Bridge	39
A Hard Day In Venice	41
Edmonton Stopover	44
March First	46
Walking Danny	47
Poem In Late Autumn	49
The Yellow Irresistible	51
Your Thirteenth Birthday	53
Perch Fishing On Lake Eden	54
Winter Graveyard, Toronto	55
Ruskin In St Mark's, Venice	56
Home Again	58
Visiting Grandfather	59
Alderson, Alberta: "Star Of The Prairie"	61

Father

on the road to Frankfurt
July of fifty eight
rounding a bend toward
a red-bricked German town
you suddenly stopped the car
ignoring mother's protests
and as the five of us watched in amazement
climbed in your immaculate black suit
through a barbed-wire fence
and jogged through swath and stubble
toward three people working in a field

my window was rolled down
and from a hundred yards
I watched negotiations;
heard high-pitched protests,
laughter, then saw you
strip off jacket, tie,
hand them to an old blue-kerchiefed woman
and taking her triple-tined pitchfork
join the other two at work

for half an hour on the road to Frankfurt
we sat and watched you stooking grain
in perfect harmony with your co-workers,
the only incongruities
your shirt of gleaming white,
the woman standing motionless like Jeeves,
your jacket folded neatly on her arm

you were on your way to give a paper
at the Max Planck Institute
on monosomic chromosomal substitution:
a scientist merely

but when you strode back to the car
brushing chaff and sunlight from your hair
you were to me at pimply seventeen
Odysseus come to claim his kingdom back

"Just the way we did it
at Charlie Comerford's in the thirties"
was all you said:
I think that was
the clearest sight I ever got of you.

Walking Home To Mayfair, January 1928

a mile back now
Keatley's milking barn,
snuffle and slow crunch
and sighing of his cows

Friday night,
the weekly wage
safe in your mitt;
smell of the barn yielding
to taste of damp half-frozen wool,
the scarf she knit wrapped twice over your face

you have laboured since dawn
and now every tenth step or so
(the average toted as you walk)
drops you through the teasing crust
in snow up to your knees;
eleven miles still to home:
on Sunday night the same trek back again

at this moment though,
under a black poplar
creaking in a pulse of air
that sends ribbons of ice
falling through starlight,
you are not refugee
farm worker, husband,
provider to those six
waiting in your sod house,
nor scarcely a breathing man
as you see

what never will be seen again —
that ridge raised by
a fieldmouse under snow,
blue shadows trapped in rabbit tracks,
the glide of a snowy owl
through the reeds above
the Frenchman's frozen slough,
and in that stillness coyote calls
— Tallis voices raised across the drifts

yes it must have been like this
some time on those nights
so quietly passed over in two lines
of Uncle's computerized family history;
and as you plough onward again
I see all around
from Spiritwood and Mildred
Robinhood and Redfield
Mullingar and Whitkow
Hawkeye and Belbutte,
men walking wrapped in their own breath —
all our weary grandfathers
carrying our lives
triumphantly toward us through
blue-black Saskatchewan night

Black Sunday, April 14th, 1935
for Walter Stemkowski

first a small wind
then a rush of birds
then the pursuing cloud

noon is so dark
the cows run home

a neighbour woman
muck oozing down her cheeks
comes whispering judgment day

hour after hour
through windows and walls
the dust pushes in,
muddying the water
fingering the bread
drawing a dark margin
round every thought

there is no choice
but drink and eat
and breathe it in:
no orifice is spared

telling us all this,
you recall with wonder
still vivid after sixty years
the calm you felt next morning
waking in that thick blanket of earth

Untitled

Leaning over this old well
I drop the snow-filled bucket
to splinter ice
a hundred feet below.
Again that shifty sky
and alerted silence;
faraway howl once more
of the night train for Saskatoon;
and again
after seventeen years
from beyond all
western mountains
you bringing
unrest upon me
as I haul
starlight and iced water
in a narrow pail.

Winter Day Near Etzikom, Alberta

cloudless sky
unending slow
invisible sifting
white on white
horizon to horizon

bored crazy at the window
she ties a red silk stocking
to the handle of her mop,
plants it in the deepest drift

lift and flutter of scarlet there
unbinds her breath a little
as half-hour by half-hour
wrists pulsing against the sill
she watches the blue shadows
of her footsteps in the snow
fade to white

Brother Drychthelm of Melrose
Ecclesiastical History of England,
book 5, chapter 12

Bede pictures you
up to your throat
in the icy Tweed
chanting prayers
through the night
then standing rigid
on the bank until
your rags have dried
against shrinking flesh,
and explains that you
abandoned your old wife
to face these trials
solely for eternal gain.

Such cynicism may satisfy
ecclesiastical historians
but many prairie winters
and their esoteric joys
suggest less calculating aims
as I look down into
the darkening eddy
where you once prayed
to the soft calling of owls;
and, old sensualist,
I cannot help
but raise my voice
with yours tonight
for I see you stand ecstatic
in this black coil

of splintered stars,
your blood cooling
pulse slowing
to the chill
of the great stream
the drift
of Orion across the January sky.

Cindy with the News from Sky

In ancient Didyma
Apollo's priestess sat
bathing feet and sacred robe
in the mystic spring
till vapour rising from her perfumed hem
filled her with the power of the god
and all the grove with cries and mutterings.

The prophet meanwhile standing by
would turn her gibberish into verse.
Most days he had it all prepared
before the Mystery commenced,
but it was hackwork and sometimes
he'd start the session with the crazy hope
that something in the way she mouthed and moaned
might stir him past his sleepy formulas.

I often think of him while hearing you
reading in your nasal high-pitched twang
the latest news of local happenings.
With all my other muses gone on leave
I turn to you night after dreary night
through all your shifts in makeup, clothes and hair
and shutting off the sound imagine you
murmuring in pentecostal tongues
the teleprompting of some hidden god.

Celebrated Visiting Poet

*"the bundle of accidents that sits
down at the breakfast table"*
    Yeats

reads one hour
as per contract

kills questions dead
with bursts of
critical jargon
fired like Raid
to still all
undergraduate buzzing
near his space

groping bedward
from the Senior Common Room
blesses the stars
his brothers
knowing
they too
stink as they twinkle

revived
breakfasted
cheque pocketed
home he hies him

no
bundle of accidents
he

Field Mouse And Grey Owl
for John Ivan

a killing in the snow at noon today

she in her tunnel of shifting blue
runs at ease between heaps of clipped grass,
steers by nose and whisker
through dark arches of tamarack root
into her tribe's special cache:
spearmint, potentilla,
licorice-root, wild tansy;
nibbles and runs on, taut-bellied

all night the other has listened,
swarthy against the revolving dark

now, from a hundred feet –
stirrings under snow

motionless but for the whispering
sun-drenched wings
she hovers,
triangulating ears fixing
precise range, direction:
crashes fist-first through the crust

twelve inches down
the little one is pierced,
dragged quivering to the light

Old Maggie On The High Level Bridge

winter comes down white,
grabs my old shack
by every loosening joint,
sends me out at midnight
onto the iron bridge

a swaying bulb
swings my shadow
over the railing
and down 200 feet
through swivelling snow

I lean hard
against iced steel,
not ready yet
to scatter and melt
in the dark stream

but itching to get
out from behind this
shivering hide still
stitched tight over
the coward coiled inside

On Lake Agnes Trail
for Linda

we didn't walk here together
but coming down alone today
loudly crunching the snow
I am halted in mid-stride

a low soughing pulse
insistent, precise
stills my breath

high above snow-burdened firs,
stroking crisply
through incandescent blue,
raven ascending the mountain
etches her dark wake on my mind

Drylands Storm
from a letter of 1926 by a woman living near Scandia, Alberta.
for and with Linda

suddenly awake
and frantic till I feel
his soft breath on my cheek
I look up from the child and see
distant lightning finger our fields

quiet black
then the storm crawls howling
toward us again over the parched dirt

pillows pushed tight
against the quivering windows;
one cracks
as hail like a trainload of gravel
thunders through the thunder overhead

3 a.m.
exhausted sleep
in the dripping kitchen
the child snug in a drawer under the table

in morning sunlight
walking through ruin
the shed blown away
I find our turkey
huddled in a drift of hailstones

not a feather on her back:
her twelve poults safe
under wings and warm belly

Evangelical Aunt

silence
tight swallowings of tea
our last half hour together

I curse again
that jealous
ever adolescent
Lear in the sky
who wrings from you
flattery and funds
that would embarrass
even a hardened politician
and compels my choice between
discipleship and bitter enmity

you open the door
and turn away

yet because
from earliest memory
you were always
kindest to me
I hesitate
caught in the soft blaze
of African violets
from your shadowed windowsill

Suburban Grave

in the still air
a clatter of pigeons

over your gravestone
a mantle of snow

on this young maple
a clutch of dead leaves
knuckled in against
the push of spring

Hoeing The Old Woman's Garden

dirt buckles over the blade
purles round the shaft
as weeds in thousands
lean and fragrantly fall:
shepherd's purse, chickweed
but especially
the succulent pigweed sproutlings

fence posts and poplars
ripple in noon heat

lying back I watch
a cloud drift across the sun;
somewhere a gopher is squeaking

a bluebottle lands on my stomach;
there's a whiff of honey from the lunch bag
and yes: a meadowlark — still here
despite the town's encroachment

I dig my shoulders deeper
into hot earth,
watch the sunflowers stirring over me
and am briefly content

New-Age Muskie Considers
A Change Of Lifestyle

> *"Isn't it about time for the armaments industry to take*
> *advantage of this peace dividend and retool for peace?"*
>   U.S. senator commenting on the end of the Cold War

I've had trouble digesting lately

funny twinges too
like the other day
when I had that duckling
almost in my teeth and suddenly
swerved aside at the killing moment

a smallish cousin from near the dock
has started nosing around my weed bed –
had to slash his tail today to move him:
word must be getting around about me

karma is the big worry –
law of moral compensation and rebirth:
settlement of outstanding debt

some weeks I butcher and swallow
twice my weight in twitching flesh

even if I could die now I shudder
to think what I'd come back as
but the sportsmen keep sending me
back down into my abbatoir:
two years to go before I'm trophy size

now they've banned the gang hooks
that took months to dissolve
from my throat and gills
and helped me feel I was paying

they're even talking of barbless hooks
to make their sport more sporting

to me this is no game:
I'm hungry all the time
and if anything moves
I can't hold back

I've tried weeds:
they just stick in my teeth

I'm trying to meditate:
my eyes can't close

it's almost certainly too late
but please
somebody
stop me

Muskellunge – the largest member of the pike family and most prized of all North American game fishes. It is sought for its aerial acrobatics and hard fight, and also because anglers hope to establish a new record by catching one exceeding 32 Kg.

St. Hugh, Bishop of Lincoln

my room has a view of your great church:
couldn't sleep all night
staring at that floodlit façade

reading your Life today
under the central tower's
stiff upward thrust
I can't help pitying that girl
(the one who wanted you)
so expertly portrayed
in all her fleshly charm
by your pious chronicler

hot with lust and shame
you grabbed a knife,
carved the muscle
from the arm which she had brushed,
and thus escaped to *macho* eunuchdom

later as boss here
you ordered the town's lepers segregated
men from women when you learned
that some were finding comfort
in what you called *calamitous pleasure*,
then took to kissing those half-eaten mouths yourself
because, as you explained,
the leper's kisses healed your troubled soul

it takes an effort to believe
it was your kind raised this miracle
we travel half the world to see:

perhaps we should applaud, discreetly,
the craziness that brought it all about

still, I can't help wishing
you were here this sunny noon
to watch with me that fortyish blonde
lounging on the grass beside the chapter house
writing postcards to her friends,
her slender naked toes curled
round the bald head of a terracotta monk –
one of a pair hunted down at bargain price
to be hauled back to her patio in Toronto

Dirty Old Man, Edmonton Schoolyard

you boast of youthful coupling
anxious hands fumbling mouthward

the girls swarm round you jeering
as your spittled lies ooze out

I fancy that your turkey neck
would look no worse for a hard twist

it is not easy for a fiftyish
fading *prikasour* to pity you

To Wordsworth, From Ontario

I
Dear William,
I'm crazy about
Westminster Bridge
but did your
early morning
include joggers?

In my suburb
solitude exists
only
on Ontario Hydro's
right-of-way.

Just now you
might enjoy it —
sloping field
under snow,
sun rising,
wind howling,
a few last stars
blinking through
the sway of
high-tension wires —
but somehow
I doubt it.

II
driving home from the cottage
I keep thinking crazy thoughts:
don't know if they're my own

out in the dark
random headlights catch forest edges,
splinters of Shield rock,
flash of some animal's eyes,
and for a moment between rock cuts
there's Venus undulating like a belly dancer
in the bosom of Boshkung Lake –
scenes from childhood,
as it was in the beginning
dozing homeward in dad's old Chevrolet

but the sky has changed:
beyond the trees and rocks,
from all horizons
the towers are winking red:
down here in a thousand cars
the obedient alerted cellphones
collar us to the electronic leash

try to imagine, William –
billions of invisible waves each instant
penetrating me from every side;
the coded carriers
of business deals and trivia,
the lusts and loves of all Ontario
from North Bay to Niagara
eddying through my nerves and brain

when you told us of the solitary bliss
we still travel to our cottages to find,
your heart and mind were pulsing
free of such electrical pollution;
that mystic Presence deeply interfused
once rolling so smoothly through your mind
is having a bumpy ride along my neurons

around the bend:
another red eye in the sky,
this one stuck in a malevolent stare

shades of the Future Shop
close about my middle age

then down the long slope toward Toronto
the cars snake in endless procession,
their glowing hemorrhoidal butts
lined up like the bums of sinners
in some old Gothic painting
pouring into the mouth of Hell

Bereavement

I
sticky July night
in the ravine

across the moon
a quivering
net of aspen

and all around
the obscene
odorous persistence
of growing things

II
above October's
lurid gold
the sky
cooling
pushing life
where I want it
where it belongs:
underground

III
minus fifteen
on the iron bridge

but the wind
is not cold enough

the valley
not empty enough

distant howl of a train
still too near

even the stars
are pressing in tonight

and somewhere under
the ice below
dark fish wait

Sanctuary

November afternoon
the slope above a pond

suddenly on a carpet
of ashblonde and gold leaves
a dog with quiet eyes
a spaniel motionless

he and two humans
separate and silent
in a circle of trees

Counterparts
1 Samuel 19, verses 9-10

hunched on the throne
fingering your spear
you glare at the young man
who plays and sings
to lift the chill from your heart

those young legs trouble you
with the stony hills of your youth;
between his thighs the seed swarms
that will crowd out your seed;
the delicate sunburned hands
make music that was once your own
and in the confident eyes
you see yourself
that day the prophet made you king

worst of all
he's got perfect control
of all the latest jargon
for snuggling up familiarly
to the – previously – unnameable
Mystery in the sky

I think of you today
as smiling before me stands
the brightest in my senior seminar
(scholarship material, undoubtedly,
my colleagues all agree)
handing in his term exam
an hour before it's due

he pities me the marking job,
wishes me, however, a pleasant holiday,
swivels his perfect designer self
and strolls to the door

already, the first paragraph parades
Derrida, Lacan, Foucault, Eagleton,
then all the latest hot-shots
at nudging and interrogating *text*
(Shakespeare or some magazine:
it's all the same: just *text*)

the crimson marker trembles
in my clammy grasp
and I fear like you Saul
I too will miss my aim.

Angina Poem

last week my heart was scanned
by the hidden eye
of a great blunt-headed bird

strapped to the table
I saw the nurse coax it into place
then set it in attendance over me
noiselessly watching
from seven pre-set positions

when that was over it let out a squawk:
definitely triumphant

we call it a gamma scanner
the doctor said today
reviewing my results;
it reads the rate at which your blood
– radioactive by injection –
infiltrates the heart's musculature;
there's clearly some obstruction
in your right coronary artery:
go on with what you're doing
but work to lower the cholesterol

I was relieved of course
– my late athletic flowering
could go on cautiously –
but he avoided eye contact
and I have this weird feeling
rasping across my innards
like the tongue of a restless cat

that during the half hour
that dark head hovered over me
something alien slipped inside,
planted itself where it shouldn't be:

I think for ease of future observation
they may have put a bar-code on my heart

The Eternal Feminine In Art
Inspired by the works of Andy Warhol

The Greeks held that a vivid dream of sex
with Aphrodite was propitious
provided that the dreamer had enjoyed it
(no mention of the goddess's response)
– a comforting and civilised belief
for men and Sapphic women of those times,
who carved those lovely images of her
with that enchanting and all-knowing smile
that bids us come through all eternity.

The bully-boys of Constantine then drove
the goddess and her priestesses to ground;
but countless saints soon found to their distress
lewd she-devils climbing into their beds;
they flogged themselves with deadly concentration,
cock and balls shrivelling under the nettles' lash:
but even then Sheela-na-gig declares
with granite-eyed and open-legged insistence
the goddess' ancient power was intact.

The Renaissance brought classier times for her,
and though she's been officially reduced
to virgin status, anyone who looks
knowingly at Titian's red madonna
will catch an answering twinkle in her eye:
she's learned something since her old Grecian phase
– especially that to more subtle tastes
a veil of mystery and suffering
adds piquancy to naked beauty's lure.

Walking through this Warhol retrospective
convinces me that Musil could be right
in claiming that our age has finally
banished the ancient force of passionate love,
dependent as it is upon belief.
These Marilyns don't have divinity
enough to raise a wanker's limp salute:
the soup can, though, might offer some relief,
its lid wide open, sprawling on its back.

Mosquitoes: Etzikom, Alberta, 1918
from a farmer's reminiscence

evening
after July's only rain

he smells smoke
runs and finds the horse snorting
crazily pounding
and the woman cursing quietly
beside a smudge fire

she stops slapping for a moment
the percheron's twitching shoulders

holds up to the man her blood-drenched palms

Whitemud Devotions

Hung over and in a fragile state
I sprawl under September trees
anchored by my fists in rotting leaves.

A gang of Anabaptists picnicking nearby
on lemonade and wieners and the Word
has hoisted me from autumn dreams
and roused thoughts of a day
when I came here as a boy at Easter dawn:
headlights flicker on the Whitemud Road
as we gather in steel-blue dusk
then climb in silence the toboggan hill
to hail – so the word goes – the risen Lord.

That passionate half hour must have been
the start of my apostasy, for when
the burning rim of our star rose
beyond a distant ridge of ice-bound trees
the shudder running up my spine could not
by any effort be connected to
those words our preacher mouthed so tunefully.

They're *fellowshipping* now in hearty games.
Again I hear that thudding
trinity of bump, set, and spike –
the shriek of Christian girls at volleyball.
It may be true, as Yeats's friend once claimed,
"Belief makes a mind abundant", but surely
only if a mind's there from the start.

Sour thoughts these from an arrogant drunk
composting in heat of Indian summer –
a man of faith who merely
happens not to credit very much.

The branches overhead like giant hands
stretch and squeeze a bit of squirming sky.
My belly gives another heave
as those old friends break out another hymn.
Marshmallow time has come: *abide with me.*

On The Old CPR Bridge

restless after the storm
I walk the rail-bed
out onto the bridge

tracks long gone,
the sleepers remain
except for this gap
a hundred feet above the ice
where a dozen are missing

snow coiling
over the dark hole
sends a tingling
through toes and soles
up into my crotch and gut
as I hesitate,
getting up nerve
to slither across
belly down, eyes forward,
hugging the narrow beam

I hear my breath,
sift of snow,
a throbbing in the ears;
but if I falter
during this
suddenly essential test,
know the note I'll carry
down to eternity
is the efficient drone

of those giant steel grasshoppers
beyond the far bank
patiently humping the prairie
for Bow Valley Pipelines Ltd.

A Hard Day In Venice

> *"In the courtyard of his palace at Peking, Kubilai Khan sowed seeds of prairie grass to remind himself of the freer world from which he had come."*
>   Ronald Latham, The Travels of Marco Polo

morning again in the beautiful city

sun burns through mist above San Giorgio;
Turner coming true once more
but the miracle's turned mundane

the Jesuits' bell on the Zattere
clanks like a pot bashed by a ladle

thrushes and blackbirds
singing from their roofgardens
are cancelled by the bull pigeons
cooing and gurgling everywhere
in their spiral rut
round the bored but nimble females,
who nonetheless are sometimes found
face down dead in a puddle,
gang-raped by San Marco's sacred birds

the beggar from Sarajevo
whimpering on the Academy Bridge
gets nothing from me today

as for the locals,
Ruskin got it right:
lizards sprawling and spitting
in the Doge's porches;
the only sentient one among them
raving at each passerby

things improve a bit in Bar di Giorgio
after a grappa-corrected coffee
and a read of the baseball scores
in the International Herald Tribune.
I manage briefly to re-convince myself
that the book I'm working on
justifies the thirty grand
it costs to keep me here

inside the Baptistery
locked in by special permission
against the other tourists
I photograph and analyse the carvings
on Dandolo's tomb,
but catch myself after an hour
gaping up at Salomé
waltzing in her polka-dot gown
with the Baptist's bloody head

by mid-afternoon
I've wandered off
to my favourite corner
in the square of San Pietro:
a small mongrel,
legs splayed against the steps,
howls at the church door;
boys attack a football;
but best of all
spreading out a hundred feet
around my rickety bench,
this dishevelled grass –
even a few glistening dog turds

for a moment I'm caught
breathless in a field
just outside Saskatoon
with mother and our pomeranian
fifty-odd years ago:
it's spring with magic
dogwood stems reflected
in a little melt pool

but soon the white tower overhead
starts booming me back
into my tired drift
past all this publishable
marble and stone
Beauty that doesn't need
anything from me

Edmonton Stopover

The photos from those years are lost.

All afternoon, circling in the rain
through our old neighbourhood,
I try to see my way back to you.

At the house I catch you
under our giant black ash
tamping its infant root-ball down
in October dusk forty years ago:
smells of rotting gunny-sack
and Saturday's baking come unsought
but your face is averted,
eyes as always on the task in hand.

Parked near your laboratory and office
I hear beyond the shuffle of the wipers
the clatter of Miss Maclean's Olivetti;
then in the shadow of closed eyes
you appear at your microscope
sketching chromosomal aberrations.
I helped you with the work two highschool summers
(those shattered nests of ruby-spotted snakes
arrested half-uncoiled in vinegar
drifted through my dreams for years after).
You wave me over
to see a unique fragmentation,
but trying to snare your look looking at me
I find only two bristling eyebrows,
then a blizzard of labcoat white.

Finally I stop outside the wooden church
where you gave those talks on Darwin
reconciled to Genesis.
Seek and ye shall find was your great text
for tackling science, life and the Almighty;
and when you suddenly lay dying
– amazed, at forty-five –
I'm told you looked the doctor in the eye,
demanded a *post-mortem*,
instructed your about-to-be widow
on friends she should contact
and said you were going home

from which I gather you may have found
what you were looking for.
But when and where will I find you
my fair-haired hidden father?
I'm ten years older than you now
returning east tomorrow
and on my rented windshield
through this fading light
the rain is falling faster.

March First

my favourite Debussy was playing
when the phone call came:
Father dying

walked
to the bottom of our street;
the dog may have come
but I recall only
pillars of vapour
over midnight houses
crunch of snow
Helgeson's great blue spruce

back in the house
La Mer played on:
third movement –
that throbbing,
foaming, thrashing,
ever since to me
your brain drowning
body convulsing
as your heart pumps the red tide
through a broken artery

but hearing again tonight
after 30 years' avoidance
this brawling of water, wind and stone,
one passage near the end
comes home to me:
a high whisper of
violins held unwavering
half a minute above the mayhem
carrying a brief promise of your peace

Walking Danny

we walk through our small town together

there's a tension between us
constant, unadjustable

you lunge against the halter
toward two squirrels flickering
through Dr Zeck's hedge

I drag you past the weed patch
behind the co-op elevator
steaming with cat piss

on the railway track
you are free to run at last
but just then Finnegan appears
sputtering for a fight but much too small

reluctantly, in the nick of time
I grab my half-wolf
would-be Controller of Small Mammals
and head for home

near the highschool a girl approaches:

frayed jeans Adidas shoes Tommy shirt
hair spray-blasted to skull
lipstick eyeshadow blush
peergroup ingroup regulation right
lip curled defiant

seeing you
her look softens:
you pull hard toward her

she doesn't pause though
nor raise her glance
nor answer the grey-haired business
at this end of the leash
who ventured hello
whose daughter lives away
and stoops and scoops
for her own dog now

Poem In Late Autumn

"The great wings sighing with a nameless hunger"
Derek Mahon, "Canadian Pacific"

Here they come again
our resident Canada Geese
circling in ragged patterns
over rooftops and parking lots
bellies aglow
in low morning sun

it's late October and the urge
to travel somewhere
has them up and gabbling
in tight return trips
to the cornfields at the edge of town

their stupid clamour
sends me out walking
nettled by thoughts
of my own long-distance dreams
shrunk to a routine circling
near the limits of the manageable

at the new subdivision
I find them settled
on and around its landscaped
all-weather pond:
neat dowels of green
gooseshit adorn the pathways

in this a modern
life-skills demonstration
on applied adaptability?
Just now at Millennium's end
when all things appear to be
as the great Willy wrote
falling apart,
our geese may have it right:
their centre seems to be
holding nicely
here at the heart of Swan Lake
Executive Estates

meanwhile high above unspoiled pasture
a mile beyond town limits
a great squadron of the untamed cousins
is straining south toward the killing fields
their congregated voices
an occasional low muttering on the wind

The Yellow Irresistible
for Phil

twilight
midges swarming
cool pressure of water
as I wade
small trout taking
my tiny brown fly

on the bank
changing patterns
in hope of
a bigger catch,
your face comes
insistently to mind
as you were when
aged nine or ten
we older brothers
let you in
on this mystery
its sacred names:

Blue Dun
White Wulff
Black Gnat
Red Ant
Brown Hackle
Grey Fox
Ginger Quill
Professor
Royal Coachman
Maggot Nymph

Silver Doctor
Woolly Bugger
Queen of the Water
Dark Montreal

soon you owned
the sweetest cast
on the river
your line rolling out
like electricity
yet dropping the fly
soft as the living thing
over a new rise

when they sent me
your fishing tackle
all those years ago
I thought I'd never touch
the exquisite flies you tied
that final winter

but tonight I can't
keep my hands off this one,
recalling your laughter
at its braggart name

Your Thirteenth Birthday
for Cathleen

Late winter storm
sky blanched in April light
gulls tack across driving snow

kildeer cry again
around the hydro towers,
birch buds start to feather out.

Perch Fishing On Lake Eden
for Mother

skin to skin nearly
with the water
I drift through morning mist

I am nine again
and you are teaching us
to lean out from the boat
like this,
look down
through our own reflections,
bob and twitch the worm,
until the almost invisible
spectre of moving stripes
emerges from the weeds,
darts, hesitates, strikes —
is jerked into air

we had cried the day before
brother and I
thrashing the water for hours
with our flashy bucktail spinners
and never a nibble

Winter Graveyard, Toronto

acres of plastic flowers
twitch in December wind

savoury onionbursts
blow down from burgerland

gravediggers' pickup truck
belches heavy metal

it's hard to feel
elegiac as I stand
over your bones
this brilliant noon

Ruskin In St Mark's, Venice:
The Stones Talk Back, January 1877

There you are again:
down from England,
notebook in hand,
measuring
my marble flanks,
watercolours
at the ready,
icy fingers
trying to coax
thin madonnas down
from my darkening gold.

Yes, there is warmth
in my alabaster limbs,
as you wrote, John,
but it is for the eyes only,
and all eyes at that.

You have left
the girl behind,
that crazy one
dead in Ireland,
and though I may be
– as you so kindly wrote –
despite these
cursed restorations
"as lovely a dream as ever
filled human imagination",

and sincerely grateful
for your protection
(not to mention
the great publicity):
I cannot be your woman.

Home Again

*"The thirteen years I spent in Toronto were not
necessarily a bad thing."*
  Andrew Davis, British conductor *

It must have been fearfully hard Andrew
living here in exile thirteen years
far from those bubs of Mother England
that nourished your remarkable
ways with a baton and with old Mahler

now happily restored to culture's *crèche*
it may be with a certain satisfaction
that you look back on your Toronto days
and those of us who, ignorant but eager,
fed our dull spirits at the TSO

we thank you humbly for your sacrifice
and are so chuffed to be assured also
that your time here was not entirely wasted —
may we expect a knighthood to delight us
when you return to grace our hall one day?

meanwhile we recall with fond affection
you in your shimmering black patent shoes
presenting your gyrating schoolboy's bum
to our colonial gaze. O for a go
with that red-hot baton: could any spot
in dear old England quench its fire more fittingly?

---

* In an interview entitled "The Man With The Red-Hot
Baton", *The Sunday Times*, 15th July, 1990.

Visiting Grandfather

Again I take the hectic road
to this quiet south Ontario town
and its Mennonite home for the aged.

At ninety-six you tire easily
but visiting is a pleasure
as we sit on your bed talking
of your young days in the Ukraine:
trips to Odessa with your father,
the watermelons, the fishing,
and how at the first nightingale
children were free to go barefoot;
then about the war and your Red Cross work
between the Whites and Reds;
the Twenties' famine and migration
by Holland and Mexico to
CPR bush in Saskatchewan
and your first winter there:
a family of seven in a sod house
finished just before freeze-up;
Dickens read aloud by kerosene lamp
to improve the family English
("We've never been as happy since.")
You tell again of that deep well
and how you almost smothered
digging at the bottom in darkness;
how they pulled you up by rope
then drew the well-gas out of there
in bucket after bucket packed with snow.

Your courtesy still humbles me:
asking about my family,
naming the children and recalling
where they last were and what doing;
your curiosity too – how is
that woeful hockey team this year,
and house prices in downtown Metro? –
all this amid untold humiliation
from your collapsing body:
but Moses still in eye and brain.

Then comes the awkward moment
when you talk, as often lately,
of your longing for death;
and I, troubled by your breathing,
tick of a clock, distant hiss
of an occasional car,
still cannot meet your eyes
nor find a truthful response.
Even in that religious calm
which makes you what you are,
which I could never share,
it must be difficult to know
what one is really thinking,
let alone trying to span
by word or look or touch
this distance fixed between us finally.

Alderson, Alberta: "Star Of The Prairie"
(founded 1910; ghost town by mid-50s)

in the burnt grass
a gopher's skull
rotted clean
washed and blown
paper thin

crimson waves
of grasshopper wings
fan out over sage and cactus
ahead of my careful steps
until, near the level crossing
among fresh gopher mounds
rabbit droppings
a rattlesnake's skin,
I find four boulders
spaced much too evenly,
a rusted gearwheel
and finally
this thin sprawl
of shattered boards

I had read of your decay
in one of Aunt's old newspapers
and feeling desolate myself
came to touch,
make your desolation mine

but surrounded today
by this hot burrowing life,
those antelope grazing

where Railway Avenue ran,
a hawk overhead,
meadowlark on the wind,
I can't suppress
a quiet joy
as I stand within these
scarcely discernible
scoops and scratchings
in the dryland dirt
where your thousand walls once rose
from their shallow dream beds